CW00530115

FRANCIS FRITH'S

MID-WALES - CEREDIGION & POWYS PHOTOGRAPHIC MEMORIES

THE FRANCIS FRITH COLLECTION

www.francisfrith.com

FRANCIS FRITH'S

MID-WALES
CEREDIGION AND POWYS

PHOTOGRAPHIC MEMORIES

MICHAEL FREEMAN began to take an active interest in archaeology and local history at the age of 13, and went on to read archaeology at Cardiff. He was an assistant in Pembrokeshire Museums for nine years before moving to Ceredigion where he has worked as assistant Curator for the County Museum for twenty years. His main interest is the interpretation of local history.

JOHN A MILNES, After a career in journalism and teaching, John Milnes is now a freelance writer on a wide variety of subjects from self-help books to local history, including several titles for the Frith Book Company.

FRANCIS FRITH'S
PHOTOGRAPHIC MEMORIES

MID-WALES
CEREDIGION
AND POWYS
PHOTOGRAPHIC MEMORIES

MICHAEL FREEMAN
AND JOHN MILNES

First published in the United Kingdom in 2004 by The Francis Frith Collection

Hardback Edition 2004 ISBN 1-85937-511-1
Paperback Edition 2009 ISBN 978-1-84589-494-8

Text and Design copyright © The Francis Frith Collection
Photographs copyright © The Francis Frith Collection

The Frith photographs and the Frith logo are reproduced under licence from Heritage Photographic Resources Ltd, the owners of the Frith archive and trademarks

All rights reserved. No photograph in this publication may be sold to a third party other than in the original form of this publication, or framed for sale to a third party. No parts of this publication may be reproduced, stored in a retrieval system, or transmitted, in any form, or by any means, electronic, mechanical, photocopying, recording or otherwise, without the prior permission of the publishers and copyright holder.

British Library Cataloguing in Publication Data

Francis Frith's Mid-Wales - Ceredigion and Powys
Photographic Memories
Michael Freeman and John Milnes
ISBN 978-1-84589-494-8

The Francis Frith Collection
Frith's Barn, Teffont,
Salisbury, Wiltshire SP3 5QP
Tel: +44 (0) 1722 716 376
Email: info@francisfrith.co.uk
www.francisfrith.com

Printed and bound in Great Britain

Front Cover: **CENARTH**, *Sheep Dipping c1960* C376035t
Frontispiece: **CRICKHOWELL**, *The Bridge 1893* 32606

The colour-tinting is for illustrative purposes only, and is not intended to be historically accurate

AS WITH ANY HISTORICAL DATABASE THE FRITH ARCHIVE IS CONSTANTLY BEING CORRECTED AND IMPROVED AND THE PUBLISHERS WOULD WELCOME INFORMATION ON OMISSIONS OR INACCURACIES

CONTENTS

FRANCIS FRITH
VICTORIAN PIONEER

FRANCIS FRITH, founder of the world-famous photographic archive, was a complex and multi-talented man. A devout Quaker and a highly successful Victorian businessman, he was philosophical by nature and pioneering in outlook.

By 1855 he had already established a wholesale grocery business in Liverpool, and sold it for the astonishing sum of £200,000, which is the equivalent today of over £15,000,000. Now a very rich man, he was able to indulge his passion for travel. As a child he had pored over travel books written by early explorers, and his fancy and imagination had been stirred by family holidays to the sublime mountain regions of Wales and Scotland. 'What lands of spirit-stirring and enriching scenes and places!' he had written. He was to return to these scenes of grandeur in later years to 'recapture the thousands of vivid and tender memories', but with a different purpose. Now in his thirties, and captivated by the new science of photography, Frith set out on a series of pioneering journeys up the Nile and to the

Near East that occupied him from 1856 until 1860.

INTRIGUE AND EXPLORATION

These far-flung journeys were packed with intrigue and adventure. In his life story, written when he was sixty-three, Frith tells of being held captive by bandits, and of fighting 'an awful mid-night battle to the very point of surrender with a deadly pack of hungry, wild dogs'. Wearing flowing Arab costume, Frith arrived at Akaba by camel sixty years before Lawrence of Arabia, where he encountered 'desert princes and rival sheikhs, blazing with jewel-hilted swords'.

He was the first photographer to venture beyond the sixth cataract of the Nile. Africa was still the mysterious 'Dark Continent', and Stanley and Livingstone's historic meeting was a decade into the future. The conditions for picture taking confound belief. He laboured for hours in his wicker dark-room in the sweltering heat of the desert, while the volatile chemicals fizzed dangerously in their trays. Back in London he exhibited his photographs and was 'rapturously cheered' by members of the Royal Society. His reputation as a photographer was made overnight.

VENTURE OF A LIFE-TIME

Characteristically, Frith quickly spotted the opportunity to create a new business as a specialist publisher of photographs. He lived in an era of immense and sometimes violent change.

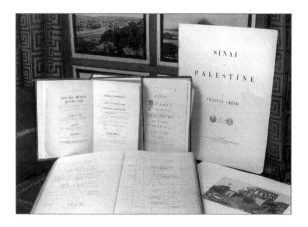

For the poor in the early part of Victoria's reign work was exhausting and the hours long, and people had precious little free time to enjoy themselves. Most had no transport other than a cart or gig at their disposal, and rarely travelled far beyond the boundaries of their own town or village. However, by the 1870s the railways had threaded their way across the country, and Bank Holidays and half-day Saturdays had been made obligatory by Act of Parliament. All of a sudden the working man and his family were able to enjoy days out and see a little more of the world.

With typical business acumen, Francis Frith foresaw that these new tourists would enjoy having souvenirs to commemorate their days out. In 1860 he married Mary Ann Rosling and set out on a new career: his aim was to photograph every city, town and village in Britain. For the next thirty years he travelled the country by train and by pony and trap, producing fine photographs of seaside resorts and beauty spots that were keenly bought by millions of Victorians. These prints were painstakingly pasted into family albums and pored over during the dark nights of winter, rekindling precious memories of summer excursions.

THE RISE OF FRITH & CO

Frith's studio was soon supplying retail shops all over the country. To meet the demand he gathered about him a small team of photographers, and published the work of independent artist-photographers of the calibre of Roger Fenton and Francis Bedford. In order to gain some understanding of the scale of Frith's business one only has to look at the catalogue issued by Frith & Co in 1886: it runs to some 670 pages, listing not only many thousands of views of the British Isles but also many photographs of most European countries, and China, Japan, the USA and Canada - note the sample page shown on page 9 from the hand-written Frith & Co ledgers recording the pictures. By 1890 Frith had created the greatest specialist photographic publishing company in the world, with over 2,000 sales outlets - more than the combined number that Boots and WH Smith have today! The picture on the next page shows the Frith & Co display board at Ingleton in the Yorkshire Dales (left of window). Beautifully constructed with a mahogany frame and gilt inserts, it could display up to a dozen local scenes.

POSTCARD BONANZA

The ever-popular holiday postcard we know today took many years to develop. In 1870 the Post Office issued the first plain cards, with a pre-printed stamp on one face. In 1894 they allowed other publishers' cards to be sent through the mail with an attached adhesive halfpenny stamp. Demand grew rapidly, and in 1895 a new size of postcard was permitted called the court card, but there was little room for illustration. In 1899, a year after Frith's death, a new card measuring 5.5 x 3.5 inches became the standard format, but it was not until 1902 that the divided back came into being, so that the address and message could be on one face and a full-size illustration on the other. Frith & Co were in the vanguard of postcard development: Frith's sons Eustace and Cyril continued their father's monumental task, expanding the number of views offered to the public and recording more and more places in Britain, as the

St Catherine's College
Senate House & Library
Gerrard Hostel Bridge
Geological Museum
Addenbrooke's Hospital
St Mary's Church
Fitzwilliam Museum, Pitt Press &c
Buxton, The Crescent
The Colonnade
Public Gardens
Haddon Hall, View from the Terrace
Miller's Dale.

coasts and countryside were opened up to mass travel.

Francis Frith had died in 1898 at his villa in Cannes, his great project still growing. The archive he created continued in business for another seventy years. By 1970 it contained over a third of a million pictures showing 7,000 British towns and villages.

FRANCIS FRITH'S LEGACY

Frith's legacy to us today is of immense significance and value, for the magnificent archive of evocative photographs he created provides a unique record of change in the cities, towns and villages throughout Britain over a century and more. Frith and his fellow studio photographers revisited locations many times down the years to update their views, compiling for us an enthralling and colourful pageant of British life and character.

We are fortunate that Frith was dedicated to recording the minutiae of everyday life. For it is this sheer wealth of visual data, the painstaking chronicle of changes in dress, transport, street layouts, buildings, housing, engineering and landscape that captivates us so much today. His remarkable images offer us a powerful link with the past and with the lives of our ancestors.

THE VALUE OF THE ARCHIVE TODAY

Computers have now made it possible for Frith's many thousands of images to be accessed almost instantly. Frith's images are increasingly used as visual resources, by social historians, by researchers into genealogy and ancestry, by architects and town planners, and by teachers involved in local history projects.

In addition, the archive offers every one of us an opportunity to examine the places where we and our families have lived and worked down the years. Highly successful in Frith's own era, the archive is now, a century and more on, entering a new phase of popularity. Historians consider the Francis Frith Collection to be of prime national importance. It is the only archive of its kind remaining in private ownership. Francis Frith's archive is now housed in an historic timber barn in the beautiful village of Teffont in Wiltshire. Its founder would not recognize the archive office as it is today. In place of the many thousands of dusty boxes containing glass plate negatives and an all-pervading odour of photographic chemicals, there are now ranks of computer screens. He would be amazed to watch his images travelling round the world at unimaginable speeds through internet lines.

The archive's future is both bright and exciting. Francis Frith, with his unshakeable belief in making photographs available to the greatest number of people, would undoubtedly approve of what is being done today with his lifetime's work. His photographs depicting our shared past are now bringing pleasure and enlightenment to millions around the world a century and more after his death.

MID-WALES
CEREDIGION AND POWYS

CEREDIGION - AN INTRODUCTION

THE COUNTY of Ceredigion, formerly Cardiganshire, is bounded by the river Teifi to the south and east, the sea to the west, the Dovey to the north, and the Plynlimon hills to the north-east. The mountains and river valleys isolated the county from the rest of Wales, so the sea provided an essential link to trading centres in north Wales and Liverpool, and in south Wales, Bristol and Ireland.

These photographs fall into two groups: the first along the Teifi, which flows for seventy miles from its source near Pontrhydfendigaid to Cardigan, visiting villages and towns along its course; and the second along the coast road from Cardigan to the Dovey at Ynyslas, with diversions off to some of the coastal villages.

All six of the main towns of the county are visited in this book. Cardigan, the first town to be

CARDIGAN, *High Street 1956* C209105

established and for many years the county town, naturally grew up around the walls of the castle, which was established by the Normans, but taken over and rebuilt in stone under Lord Rhys from 1171. Aberystwyth was founded at the same time that Edward I decided to build a new castle there in 1277; Lampeter began as a tiny settlement around a Norman castle, and would have remained a small market town had a college not been built there in 1827. Tregaron started as a compact Welsh town built around a mediaeval church, and became an important meeting place for drovers; New Quay was a maritime town that grew as a result of a successful ship building industry - unlike the other towns, the railway never reached it. Finally, Aberaeron was a new, planned town built from about 1807.

The settlements along the Teifi are quite different in character, but most are important river crossings. Cenarth, Llandysul, Newcastle Emlyn (strictly in Carmarthenshire but with Adpar as an outpost in Ceredigion), Lampeter, Tregaron

and Pontrhydfendigaid near the more famous Strata Florida Abbey were all quite isolated until the road system was improved at the end of the 18th century. Wheeled vehicles were rare in Ceredigion until then. Even after the railway came during the mid 1860s (Ceredigion was the last county in Wales to be connected to the network), many villages remained isolated, so Welsh language and culture survived.

However, these photographs do not illustrate that survival, and indeed, they could not, although a few views show that ancient traditions such as the use of coracles did survive in Ceredigion longer than in most places. Many of the photographs are dated between the 1920s and 1960s, when progress brought cars, minor road improvements and petrol stations, and this is evident in the examples selected. The effect of the influx of holidaymakers, particularly between the wars, is also illustrated. Some of the views are very general, showing landscapes that were only just beginning to be changed by housing developments, mainly for in-comers. By the

YNYSLAS, *The Golf Course 1938* 88375

time that these photographs were taken, the major changes – road improvements and the coming of the railways; the decline of shipping and lead mining; the late Victorian growth of villages, particularly around new chapels; and the erection of a network of telegraph poles - had taken place. Yet to come were the bigger improvements to the road system; edge-of-town shopping facilities; large housing estates; and the proliferation of street furniture and signs, (as well as the ubiquitous yellow lines), few of which are present in these images.

The photographs show little of the main industry of the county, which is agriculture; by the time they were taken, the second most important industry, seafaring, particularly ship-building and its ancillary crafts, had all but died out. Lead mining, too, is not represented; but tourism, now of great importance, has clearly made its mark.

The first visitors came to Cardiganshire from about 1780 for one of two reasons. Some came in the spirit of adventure as part of a longer journey: they came to be impressed by, to draw and to paint the wild, natural landscapes, to study the customs, culture and language of the local population as if it were a foreign country, and to visit the antiquities. Others came to improve their health by bathing in the sea and taking walks, and to socialise and to 'dissipate their cares and fortunes'. Only the gentry could afford to do this.

The poor road system, the lack of good maps, and the fact that most visitors could not under-stand Welsh (even if the inhabitants knew the road to distant towns), meant that the travellers were normally restricted to the two main routes – the coast road, and the road to Aberystwyth from the east through Rhayader and the Devil's Bridge. This restricted the development of tourism to those places which could provide for the needs of these visitors – places to stay, sea bathing, and entertainments of various kinds. Only Aberystwyth was able to provide all the facilities that the visitors needed in around 1800, when the first visitors came in significant num-bers, and it was not until the middle of the 19th century that other places began to provide them,

BORTH, *Beach 1892* 30253

always on a much smaller scale.

Several factors changed the sort of people that came to Ceredigion as tourists. The first was the spread of the railway system: this brought large numbers of people on Sundays, on special excursions, and week- or fortnight-long holidays. The cheapness of this new form of transport enabled the working classes to visit the sea and countryside more easily, while the increased number of paid holidays enabled them to do so more often. After the First World War, this was accompanied by a more relaxed attitude to leisure by some, and a serious interest in camping, hiking, climbing and other outdoor pursuits by others. Aberystwyth satisfied the former, while the coastal villages in particular satisfied the latter. The increasing number of regular bus and coach journeys and the coming of private cars enabled those who could afford them to travel more widely and 'get away from it all'. Rural and coastal Ceredigion provided much that these people wanted: beautiful scenery, interesting culture and traditions, and a clean, quiet environment.

Thus a certain small sector of tourists made their way to rural Ceredigion, and this was the salvation for some of the villages. They provided a seasonal income for farmers and others who provided accommodation (including camping and caravan sites); they spent their money in the village shops (purchasing items such as the post-cards for which these photographs were taken); and they paid for a variety of entertainments and activities (such as boat trips) that kept others employed. Studies of the history of some of the villages and towns show that not only were old houses being improved, but new houses were being built during a period of population decline (the population of the county reached a peak in 1871 and became smaller each decade until 1961).

The pictures do not show many people, and those that are included are more often than not incidental, but nevertheless welcome. They are shown in their day-to-day clothes or dressed for holidays, not in formal poses for the camera; it is somewhat surprising that the smartest people are the farmers at Tregaron following their sheep to market.

NEW QUAY, *Church Street 1932* N151027

THE TEIFI VALLEY

CARDIGAN, *The Bridge c1965* C209140

An earth and timber castle was established here by the Normans in 1110. After several attempts, the Welsh took it in 1165, rebuilt it in stone and held the first Eisteddfod within its walls in 1176. The bridge is on the site of a medieval one, near which Archbishop Baldwin held a service to attract volunteers for the third Crusade in 1188. The castle wall stands below the trees on the left, and beyond it is St Mary's Church, which stood near a medieval priory.

15

CARDIGAN, *High Street 1931* C209055

This stretch of the High Street is wider than the rest, probably
because the market was originally held here; the market was
moved into the Guild Hall with its clock tower on the left,
designed by Withers in 1858-60, and considered to be a very fine
example of a multi-use public building. It contained a school, a
market and a corn exchange. The clock tower was added in 1892.

CARDIGAN
High Street 1956
C209105

The medieval street pattern still survives. Until about 1800, most of the houses would have had only two stories. Visitors to the town would have stayed in one of the few inns, such as The Black Lion on the right.

CARDIGAN, *High Street c1965* C209122

This busy scene illustrates how Cardigan became an important market town. The architecture of Cardigan is distinct from other towns in Ceredigion: many buildings were constructed from cut slate slabs from local quarries, or from different-coloured bricks from the nearby brick works. The brick works also produced ornate tiles that were used to decorate the buildings - some of these are just visible on W H Smith's building on the left.

◀ **GWBERT-ON-SEA**
The Cliff Hotel c1940
G172005

This somewhat isolated hotel near Cardigan was built to provide visitors with magnificent views of the sea and Cardigan Island, where seals and porpoises are to be seen frequently. Nearby are other isolated houses, some of which would have been leased out to visitors.

◄**CARDIGAN**
Coracles c1965
C209176

The skill of coracle navigation is being demonstrated on the Teifi, just below Cardigan bridge. In the 19th century, vast numbers were in use on this stretch of the river in summer time for salmon fishing. The quay and the large warehouses in the background are evidence that the port was one of the most important in Wales during the early 19th century.

▲ **GWBERT-ON-SEA,** *Poppit Sands 1956* G172109

The Teifi begins its journey to the sea 70 miles away; it provided an inland route for the Normans to service the castles of Cardigan and Cilgerran. It becomes very shallow at this broad and sandy estuary, restricting boat movements to a brief period at high tide. However, the sands provide a good place to fish with nets, as we can see in the middle right. In 1938 the shallow-drafted motor vessel the *West Coaster* was especially built at Cardigan to cross this shallow bar.

◄**GWBERT-ON-SEA**
Mwnt Church c1965
G172111

This isolated church near a beautiful beach was probably established during the 6th century, but not built in stone until after 1300. It is one of only a few churches in the county untouched by the Victorian restorers, and like many of the originals has only a bellcote and is painted white.

CENARTH
Sheep Dipping c1960
C376035

Cenarth, on the Teifi, is set in a spectacular gorge with a number of waterfalls, and is famous as one of the last places in Britain where licensed coracles were used, both for salmon fishing and (as we see in this view) sheep dipping. Coracles are made on a willow frame. They were originally covered with horse or ox hide, but since the late 19th century cheaper canvas or calico has been used, which needs only a single coat of pitch to make them waterproof.

▶ **LLANDYSUL**
The Church 1898
41697

Llandysul was an important Dark Age and medieval settlement, and the 13th-century church tower exemplifies this. There are a number of pre-Norman and medieval inscribed stones inside the church, which, unusually for a Ceredigion church, has both nave and aisles. The village was an important centre for weaving, but is now more famous for white water canoeing.

◀ **NEWCASTLE EMLYN**
From the Castle Ruins 1932 N118003

The castle was constructed by the Welsh in a loop of the river as a 'new castle' in 1240. In 1287 a siege engine was dragged by 40 oxen to Newcastle Emlyn from Dryslwyn, where it was joined by a large Norman army to quell a rebellion by the Welsh. We do not know what damage it did, but it was not responsible for the present state of the building, which was rebuilt as a mansion in Tudor times.

▲ **LAMPETER,** *St David's College, Old Buildings c1955* L204024

Lampeter was established as a Norman settlement, but it remained a very small place until the 1820s, when it was decided to build a theological college here. The college was built around a quadrangle like those at Oxford, and was opened in 1827.

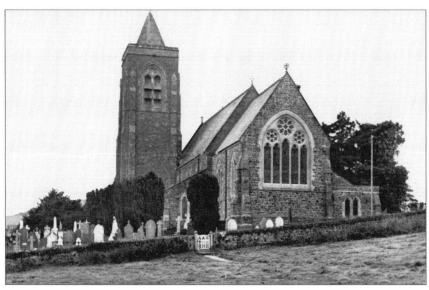

◄ **LAMPETER**
The Church c1955
L204023

The name Lampeter derives from Llanbedr, or St Peter's, to whom this church is dedicated. It is the third church on the site; this one was designed by R J Withers in 1867. Few of the late 18th- and early 19th-century visitors to the county passed through Lampeter, but one visitor who walked from Carmarthen to Chester stayed a weekend in the town in 1836. He noted how well and fashionably the people were dressed as they walked to church.

LAMPETER
High Street c1955
L204028

The arrival of the railway in 1866 gave this market town a boost, and it rapidly developed to serve a large hinterland. In the past, this part of the street was packed with horses for the annual horse fair, Ffair Dalis, which was held in early May. This view shows a wide range of shops including a jeweller, an optician, a chemist, a shoe shop, and cafes and inns.

▶ **TREGARON**
*The View from the
East 1933* T187013

Tregaron is a small
nucleated town, probably
based on a Welsh
maerdref where the lord
held court. It grew
rapidly during the early
19th century, when it
became a popular
meeting place for
drovers. The railway took
this trade away after it
arrived in 1866, but it
brought other advantages
for the local population.
The medieval church
tower rises in the centre,
and one of the two large
non-conformist chapels
stands to its right. The
town also had two
primary schools, one run
by the church, the other
by the chapel. The former
is now the popular Red
Kite Centre and Museum.

◀ **TREGARON**
*The View from the
Church Tower c1965*
T187059

On the right is a half-
timbered building that
houses a bank. The short-
lived Aberystwyth and
Tregaron bank was
established in 1810, and the
Black Ox bank (Banc y
Eidon Du), based in
Llandovery, opened a
branch in Tregaron in 1903.
Both of these were
established to save the
drovers carrying large sums
of money with them on
their return journeys from
the markets in England.

▲ **TREGARON,** *The Foot of the Pass 1933* T187017

This is the Abergwesyn pass through the mountains to the east of Tregaron. Along this road passed thousands of cattle with 'cues', or two-part iron shoes, on their feet, along with sheep, pigs and geese, the latter with their feet dipped in tar and sand. They walked to the Welsh border and beyond, where they were fattened ready for sale to English markets. This route was chosen because it had no expensive toll gates.

◄ **TREGARON**
Pony Trekking 1963
T187053

As the importance of farming declined, and woollen stockings – the main product of the women of Tregaron – were no longer wanted, the local population began to find other means of making an income. One of these was to organise pony treks for those that really wanted to get away from it all.

TREGARON
Market Day 1933
T187005

Although flocks of sheep and herds of cattle no longer congregated at Tregaron ready for the walk to England, the town continued to serve as a market place for livestock for many years. Ffair Caron was held for three days in March, while there were sheep fairs in June and September and hiring fairs in November. Here, farmers smartly dressed in three-piece suits follow one of the flocks to market.

► **TREGARON**
Pont Eynon 1933 T187001

Just to the west of Tregaron lies a vast bog, known as Cors Caron. This was once a lake that gradually filled with plants on which sphagnum moss grew. As the plants died, peat formed, which became a major source of fuel for the local inhabitants. The bog is now protected. Pont Eynon is on the edge of the bog, and crosses a stream that flows through it. It may be named after Eynon Sais, the abbot of Strata Florida in 1281.

PONTRHYDFENDIGAID
The River and the Bridge c1900 P211017

Pontrhydfendigaid means 'bridge of the blessed ford', and this is that bridge. By it is the village shop. It benefited from the visitors who came to see the nearby ruins of Strata Florida, particularly after the railway arrived in 1866, and more recently from those who came to the enormous hall in the village that was endowed by Sir David James for Eisteddfodau.

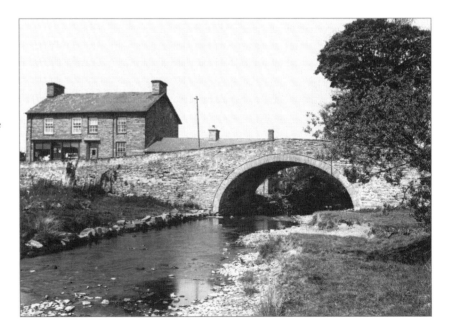

PONTRHYDFENDIGAID
The Memorial c1950
P211019

Here we have a view of the broad main street, with St David's Church and the church hall on the left. In front of them stands the fine war memorial.

PONTRHYDFENDIGAID
*Strata Florida Abbey
Ruins c1950* P211010

Strata Florida was originally
established in this remote spot
by the Normans in 1163, but
when Lord Rhys took control
of most of Ceredigion, he re-
established the abbey on a
new site, where Cistercian
monks spent about 50 years
building one of the first stone
buildings in the county. The
abbey was dissolved by Henry
VIII in 1539 and was sold to
the Earl of Essex and his
agent, John Stedman, whose
family later used much of the
stone in their mansion and
farm buildings.

PONTRHYDFENDIGAID, *The Teifi Pools c1960* P211029

This is the source of the Teifi, famous for trout and eels. The pools were mentioned by Leland, Henry VIII's librarian, when
he travelled around the country in 1536; he also noted that the surrounding land had been cleared of forest for charcoal.
The pools were mentioned in many recent local guidebooks as a popular place for fishermen.

TRAVELLING NORTH FROM CARDIGAN

ABERPORTH, *The Bay c1955* A185009

This bay is typical of a number along the coast of Ceredigion. Deeply inset, it provided shelter for loading and discharging cargoes, including herring, and for the 11 ships that were built here. From the inter-war years its fine sandy beaches attracted visitors who wanted a sea-side holiday without the distractions that resorts such as Aberystwyth provided, even though it was close to the Ministry of Defence establishment and airstrip, which were established in the late 1930s.

▼ **ABERPORTH,** *The Bay c1955* A185058

This view shows the headland that separates the two bays. The northern (further) bay
penetrates well inland and provided good shelter for boats, with limekilns, storehouses and
coal yards nearby. The beach was used once a year by farmers from Llechryd for a feast.

► **TRESAITH**
*From the Cliff Walk
c1955* T361011

This is another small bay
with good shelter and fine
sands - here only two boats
were built. Until the 1850s
there was just an inn and a
cottage in the bay, with a
limekiln nearby. It became
such a popular resort at the
end of the 19th century that
it became known as the
second Brighton.

◄**LLANGRANOG**
The Beach c1955
L263042

Llangranog has a small, sheltered bay with a sandy beach on which about 20 ships were built during the 19th century. Like Tresaith, it became popular with holidaymakers from the 1930s. On the horizon is one of a number of exposed coastal Iron Age defended settlement sites that are to be found along the coast of Ceredigion.

► **LLANGRANOG**
General View
c1955 L263039

The bus (standing by the Ship Inn, centre) was an essential service for the inhabitants, many of whom would not have had cars in the 1950s. It wound its way along the narrow roads to the main road, on the horizon, and from thence to Cardigan.

▼ **LLANGRANOG,** *The Ship Inn c1955* L263096

This inn used to provide sustenance for the boat builders, seamen and lime burners, but it soon became an important attraction for the holidaymakers.

► **LLANGRANOG**
General View c1960
L263054

There were several warehouses here; they stored domestic items brought by boat, including one called Y Storws Llestri (the Earthenware Warehouse), that contained ceramics from the Buckley potteries in north Wales.

◀ **LLANARTH**
Main Street
c1960 L255042

Llanarth was an important medieval settlement, and the church contains a pre-Norman inscribed stone. The post office on the left probably sold most basic needs, including engine oil, while the Mother's Pride van in the distance provided a home delivery service. Car drivers using the shop, post box or phone (on the left) must have caused an obstruction on this narrow part of the main road, and since this photograph was taken, the house on the right was demolished to widen it.

▶ **LLANARTH**
The Bridge and the
Post Office c1955
L255023

This view, taken from the opposite direction to L255042, above, shows the old narrow bridge more clearly. The buildings on the left have now all gone, along with the enamelled sign for 'Spillers Shapes for all dogs', but the post office is still there, now with a new telephone box.

◄ **NEW QUAY**
The Harbour 1939
N151103

New Quay became an important ship-building settlement from the late 18th century (244 ships were built here between 1779 and 1882), and since it was well protected from south-westerly gales, it was one of the few places along the coast where larger ships could shelter during storms. The three terraces of houses provided accommodation for ship builders and ancillary workers.

◄ **LLANARTH**
*The Llanina
Hotel c1955*
L255005

This hotel was
probably first built
at the end of the
18th century, when
the Turnpike Trusts
began to improve
the county's roads.
Llanarth became an
important stopping
place for those
travelling by horse
or foot along the
coast road. The
hotel later provided
another service for
travellers – BP petrol
from the three tall
cylinders by the
door (left). The
building looks the
same today, but it
has fewer chimneys.

▲ **NEW QUAY,** *The Harbour c1935* N151069

This view from the end of the stone pier shows the four-storey Custom House surrounded by
rowing boats, which were used by both local fishermen and holidaymakers. Fishing was an
important local industry, particularly during the 18th century when vast shoals of herring came
in the autumn. New Quay now serves a few local fishing boats and many leisure boat owners; a
regatta is held annually, which dates back to 1868.

◄ **NEW QUAY**
*The Coastguard
Station 1933* N151053

New Quay had a RNLI
lifeboat from 1864, and
there were coastguards
based here for the
protection of passing
boats and unfortunate or
irresponsible visitors.
Beyond the coastguard
station is the pier, built
in 1835 with stone from
a nearby quarry – the
stone was brought here
on a tramway.

NEW QUAY
Church Street 1932
N151027

▼ **NEW QUAY,** *Church Street c1950* N151135

These views (below and pages 40-41) up and down Church Street would have been familiar to Dylan Thomas, who lived near New Quay in 1944, and to many visitors, who have to park their cars at the top of the hill. New Quay featured in the 1920s film *Torn Sails*, which was based on the novel by the local author Allen Raine.

► **NEW QUAY**
The Lighthouse 1936
N151095

The stone quay and the lighthouse, known locally as the Pepperpot, were built in 1835, replacing a timber 'new quay' built in the 1690s. The pier and lighthouse were partly destroyed in the 'Royal Charter' storm of 1859, and the lighthouse was completely destroyed by a storm in 1937.

◄ **NEW QUAY**
Two Bays from
Barham House
c1930 N151047

This view shows Cei Bach (Little Quay), where a number of boats were built, with the typical Ceredigion coast beyond. Along the bay there were a number of limekilns that converted limestone from Pembrokeshire into lime suitable for improving the local acid soil or for use in mortar or whitewash.

► **NEW QUAY**
New Road showing
Gilfachreda c1935
N151050

Gilfachreda is situated on the road between New Quay and the main coast road. The road may well have been built or widened to ease the transport of caravans to New Quay.

43

NEW QUAY
The Terraces c1940
N151104

When a parson visited New Quay in 1885, he thought he had found paradise, partly because the place was so isolated. Although there were plans to make it a major port for journeys to Ireland, it was never connected to the railway network, but it became a popular holiday resort from the 1870s.

◄ **ABERAERON**
Main Street c1955
A182049

Nearly all the buildings we see here were built in the Georgian period, and they now look most attractive painted in different colours.

◀ **ABERAERON**
*The Town and
the Beach c1955*
A182031

In 1800, Aberaeron
was little more than
a farm and inn by
the main coast road
where a bridge
crossed the Aeron.
Local gentry
applied for an Act
of Parliament to
allow them to build
a new town and to
develop the
harbour, and work
began in 1807,
when the grid of
streets was laid out.

▲ **ABERAERON,** *Market Street c1955* A182068

In this street, many of the original features of the Georgian buildings, such as small shop
windows, have been retained; the wide streets of Aberaeron are a distinct contrast to most
others in the county.

◀ **ABERAERON**
Market Street c1965
A182260

Aberaeron is almost in the
middle of the 60-mile
coastline of Ceredigion. It
is now home of the main
county offices, replacing
the ancient capital,
Cardigan, and the more
recent administrative
centre, Aberystwyth. The
very top of the Town Hall
that used to house the
Council Chamber is
visible on the right.

▶ **ABERAERON**
The Harbour c1955
A182035

The original plan for building the town included a harbour, which provided a large and safe place for coastal vessels and fishing boats. From early in the 19th century, boats with visitors and goods from elsewhere along the coast made Aberaeron their destination, if only for a day trip.

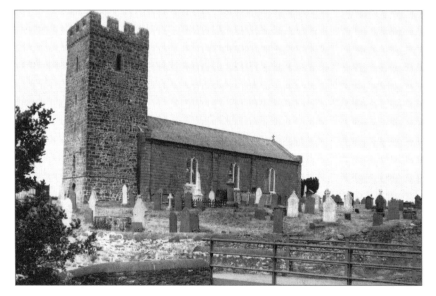

◀ **LLANON**
St Bridget's Church c1955 L265010

The church at Llanon is dedicated to St Bridget, an Irish saint, whereas the village is named after Non, the mother of St David. The church tower was built during the 14th century, but the nave was completely rebuilt during the 18th century; it is more like a chapel interior, with a big open space lit by large windows. The main road used to pass very close to the church by the sea, but it was washed away and moved inland, leaving the church rather isolated.

▲ **LLANRHYSTUD,** *General View c1960* L266072

Llanrhystud is overlooked by an Iron Age fort, just out of view on the left, which was later occupied
by Welsh and Norman earth and timber castles. A row of houses was built on the old road to
Lampeter and another on the street to the church (visible on the right). The church was built by
R K Penson in 1852, and it has one of the few spires in the county.

◀**LLANRHYSTUD**
The Square c1955
L266032

The bridge over the Wyre
became the focal point for
public houses and shops
soon after the bridge was
built (or rebuilt) in 1801,
when the Martyn family,
on a trip around Wales,
nearly came to grief
crossing the incomplete
bridge in the dark. On the
right are some aluminium
milk churns - these were a
common sight until the
introduction of bulk milk
tankers in the 1980s

ABERYSTWYTH
North Parade 1949
A14285

At the beginning of the 19th century, a number of new streets were built following the grid pattern of the mediaeval town. North Parade was one of these, but it was made much wider than the others to allow the local militia to use it as a parade ground. The National Provincial Bank of England on the left was built in 1901-03 on the site of the first houses to be built outside the medieval town walls in 1797. Chalybeate Street on the right led to the chalybeate well, which was used by visitors who came to drink its waters.

ABERYSTWYTH, *The Castle Grounds 1921* 71524

Here we see the interior of the castle, built by Edward I between 1277 and 1289. Very little survives, because Cromwell ordered its destruction in 1649, and locals used it as a quarry until it became an attraction for early visitors to the town. In the centre is a circle of stones set up in 1914 for the 1915 National Eisteddfod (delayed for a year owing to the First World War). In the foreground is the site of the well - it was found to be sixty feet deep.

ABERYSTWYTH, *The Beach 1899* 44526

Aberystwyth became a popular resort for the well-off, who came
here to bathe and socialise from the late 18th century. Once the
railway arrived in 1864, many more visitors came; a variety of
activities was arranged for them, including bathing from the
bathing machines in the middle of the picture, taking trips
around the bay in the rowing or sailing boats, or being
entertained at the top of Constitution Hill (in the background).

▶ **ABERYSTWYTH**
The College
1899 44528

The magnificent neo-Gothic building on the prom began life as a triangular house designed by John Nash in about 1795. In 1865 the railway entrepreneur Savin began to build the Castle Hotel around it, but he became bankrupt in the process. It was bought by the fledgling University in 1872, who made several alterations to it over the next 25 years; in 1901 they agreed to allow the Town Council to build a promenade around it, so long as the students were not disturbed by entertainers.

◀ **ABERYSTWYTH**
Rough Sea c1930
A14010

Here we see the College buildings after the new prom was built in 1901-04. This wonderful location must have been rather distracting for the students of 'The College by the Sea'. Storms are frequent along the coast, but these buildings are protected from the worst by Castle Point, from which this view was taken.

▲ **ABERYSTWYTH,** *From Constitution Hill 1897* 39396

This is a very popular view of the town, showing the three bays separated by rock outcrops. The pier was built on one of these outcrops in 1865, only to be damaged in a storm the following year. On the left at the end of the Prom is a hut used by the builders of the second part of Alexandra Hall, which housed women students. They had to walk to the college at the other end of the Prom several times a day.

◀**ABERYSTWYTH**
The Vale of Rheidol Railway 1903 49500

This 12-mile-long railway was constructed along the south side of the Rheidol in 1901 to transport lead ore from the mines to the harbour, but it became a very popular tourist attraction for those wishing to visit the Devil's Bridge and waterfalls where the line terminated. This view shows a cutting and embankment that is typical of this steep valley-side line.

▼ **DEVIL'S BRIDGE,** *The Falls c1880* 13280

This view shows the 'sublime horrors' of the waterfall that the first visitors came to see: the hotel provided for their needs. One visitor wrote in 1797: 'Language is but ill calculated to convey an accurate idea of the scene which is here presented to the eye. The awful height of the fissure which the bridge bestrides a hundred feet above the observer, rendered doubly gloomy by its narrowness, and the wood which overhangs it; the stunning noise of the torrent thundering at his feet, and struggling through black opposing rocks, which its ceaseless impetuosity has worn into shapes strange and grotesque fill the mind with a mingled but sublime emotion of astonishment, terror and delight.'

▶ **DEVIL'S BRIDGE**
The Falls c1940 D140156

The English name associates the bridge with a story in which the devil is tricked, while the Welsh name (Pontarfynach) suggests that it was built by the monks of Strata Florida. There are now three bridges. The first is possibly medieval; the second was built in 1753, but improved in 1814; and the last was built by the County Council in 1901. Nearly 10,000 people visited the site in 1865 - hence the need for steps and railings.

◀ **TALYBONT**
General View
c1955 T185009

This compact village is situated on the main coast road north of Aberystwyth; it grew up to serve the workers of the nearby lead mines and woollen mills. In addition to the inns, there were several chapels (one is visible on the hill slope near the middle of the picture) and a church (top right). The large building in the middle was a warehouse that provided the farmers and miners with all their requisites.

▶ **TALYBONT**
The Square c1960
T185045

The two public houses on the square (The Black Lion and The White Lion) provided rest and refreshment for travellers and those who visited the fairs that were held on the land in front of them.

◄ DOLYBONT
The Village c1940
D262093

This small village had a café, the Dolybont Café (centre), whose sign was visible from the road between Talybont and Borth – the proprietors hoped that holidaymakers would stop on their way to or from the beach. In the distance is the large roof of the Calvinistic Methodist Capel y Babell, built in 1874.

◄ **TALYBONT**
*Middle
Talybont c1960*
T185057

The shop and garage stand on what is now a busy main road.

▲ **CLARACH BAY,** *1921* 71529

Clarach consists of dispersed settlements in a fertile valley to the north of Aberystwyth, from which it is accessible by foot over Constitution Hill. Having made the energetic walk, visitors were greeted by a café and a secluded beach. At the far end is a farm whose land was once owned by Welsh princes and Norman kings.

◄ **BORTH**
The Beach 1892
30253

Much of Borth consists of a single street with houses on both sides that gradually spread between the railway station at the north end of the village to a group of fishermen's houses built in the lee of a promontory at the south end – we can see the remains of one of them on the left. St Matthew's Church, visible in the distance, was built on higher ground. The larger buildings are a school and chapel.

59

▼ **UPPER BORTH,** *1906* 57126

This is the original nucleus of Borth village from which picture No 30253 was taken (page 59). Some of these houses were owned by sea captains, who could afford to build a substantial two-story house. It is said that almost every boy from Borth went to sea. In the foreground are some fine clinker-built fishing boats.

► **BORTH**
Cambrian Terrace
1938 88372

This is the first view that many visitors would have had of Borth. It was taken from the railway station, which was built in 1863 when the Cambrian Railway arrived on its way from Machynlleth to Aberystwyth. On the left are a number of shops hoping to catch the eye of the passing visitor on their way to or from the beach. On the right is the massive Grand Hotel, one of three built by Savin, who also built the railway station.

◀ **BORTH**
*Cambrian Terrace
1899* 44581

The elegant brick railway station is at the far end, and the Grand Hotel is on the left. On the right is the Taliesin Hotel. When the row of houses next door to it was built in the 1860s, it must have almost doubled the population of the village. The shop sold postcards, and displays model yachts in the doorway for sailing on one of the pools on the beach.

▶ **BORTH**
*The Parade and
the Beach 1899*
44535

This parade of large shops and houses are just round the corner from the station. The pebbly storm beach gives way to a vast fine sandy beach, covered in this photograph by a high tide. On the right is a tent and small wind shelters, while further along is a solitary bathing machine, which appears never to have been moved down to the sea.

◄ **BORTH**
The Beach 1921 71541

This view, with the Grand Hotel on the left, shows the extent of the beach. The girls are wearing light short dresses - quite a contrast to their Victorian and Edwardian predecessors, who wore several layers of clothes, even on the beach. Beneath the sand is the remains of a forest that grew here at the end of the Ice Age before the sea rose to its present level. The stumps of massive trees, and the peat they grew in, are sometimes exposed by heavy seas.

◀ **BORTH**
The Beach 1925
77766

Children play at
the south end of
the beach. Beyond
them is the
headland on which
the Borth war
memorial was built
after the First
World War. There
are said to be
smugglers' caves in
the rocks below it.

▲ **BORTH,** *High Street 1952* B147211

This busy street has many shops and cafes to serve both the locals and visitors, but some close
for the winter. The shops and houses on the left back straight on to the sea.

◀ **BORTH**
High Street c1955
B147170

The Friendship Hotel
(right) was named after a
ketch owned by a ship's
captain when he started
selling drinks on the
premises in 1860. The lack
of vehicles and yellow
lines is quite a contrast to
today's busy scene (but
note the No Waiting sign
on the right)

► **BORTH**
Brynowen Farm Caravan Park
c1960 B147243

This view illustrates the three main occupations of the people of Borth – seafaring, farming, and tending to the needs of holidaymakers. A number of caravan sites were established in Borth after the Second World War, multiplying the population of the village in summer by many times its winter number.

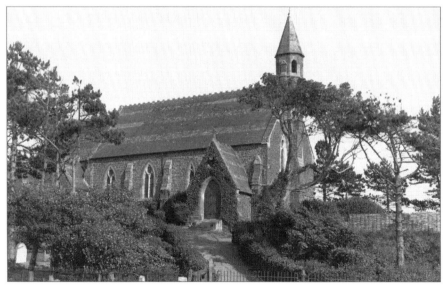

◄ **BORTH**
St Matthew's Church
c1950 B147201

St Matthew's Church was built on a hillock a few hundred yards inland from Borth. When it was consecrated by the Bishop of St David's in 1876, music was provided by the pupils of Upping School, Rutland, 300 of whom stayed in Borth for nine months to escape a fever prevalent in the school and from which some of their fellows had died. Their offer to build a road to the church was declined.

▲ **YNYSLAS,** *The Sand Dunes 1933* 85718

To the north of Borth lies Ynyslas, which consists of a fine series of sand dunes, many now protected as a National Nature Reserve. Here, during the Second World War, secret rockets and radar bugging devices were tested, and a number of brick and concrete buildings were erected to protect those observing the experiments.

◄**YNYSLAS**
The Golf Course 1938
88375

Just inland of the sand dunes is a golf course - it was established in 1885, and may be the oldest in Wales. Beyond it is possible to see the Dovey and the hills of Merionethshire.

POWYS - AN INTRODUCTION

POWYS could be considered a new county – it existed only after the 1974 Local Government Act, which brought wholesale re-organisation to the counties of Wales. The older folk may talk dismissively about Powys, remembering the good old days of the three counties of Breconshire (Brecknockshire in full), Radnorshire and Montgomeryshire, which make up the current county. But one thing to remember about Wales is to take nothing at face value - little in this wonderful country is as it seems.

Powys takes its name from an older Dark Age kingdom. Its origins are indeed obscure, but it certainly existed by the 9th century. The meaning of the word 'Powys' is clouded with uncertainty. Perhaps the most likely definition comes from the Latin 'pagenses', translated as 'dwellers in the countryside'. By 1536, under the Act of Union of Henry VIII the various Welsh kingdoms were finally abolished and replaced with counties along English lines. For the first time Montgomeryshire, Radnorshire and Breconshire appeared as units of local government. The first Powys disappeared, and would not be known again till 1974.

It is hard to describe the landscape of Powys without an overuse of superlatives. The scenery here is something special, with rolling countryside all the way from the wide open spaces of the Brecon Beacons National Park in the south to the wild beauty of the Berwyn Mountains in the north. Between these two mountain ranges lie the calmer and smoother lakes of the Elam Valley and the massive Lake Vyrnwy, the rolling, timeless landscapes along the border, the multitude of rivers and mountain streams, the characterful country towns and villages, and a rich history which embraces everything from stone circles and other mysterious prehistoric monuments to Victorian spa towns.

Powys is the least-populated county of Wales, with a community of 121,000; covering an area of 2,009 square miles, it has one of the lowest population densities in Northern Europe. Llandrindod Wells, with a population of 5,000, is the administrative centre, and it is also a spa town with magnesium, sulphur and chalybeate springs. Welshpool (population 6,000) holds the Crown Court, and in typically contrary fashion, the police force of Dyfed – Powys police has its headquarters in Carmarthen!

In the north west of the county, the heather-covered Berwyn Mountains rise to 2,713 feet; to the west are the rounded grassy slopes of Plynlimon (in Welsh Plumlumon or Pumlumon Fawr), 2468 feet high. In the south are the Brecon Beacons, the highest mountains in South Wales, and also the Black Mountains. The Brecon

Beacons are made up primarily of red sandstone, and rise in places to over 2,000 feet. They also contain a considerable limestone area, which contains, at 12 miles, the longest continuous cave system in Britain. The limestone geology also gives us numerous spectacular waterfalls. To the north of the Beacons is Radnor forest, a treeless moorland, which rises steeply to 2,165 feet above the fertile lowlands.

Powys is still mainly agricultural: sheep graze on the upland slopes and cattle are fattened on the lowland pastures, while cereal crops are grown in the river valleys. The only old industry still struggling on is the mining of granite, slate and limestone around Welshpool. The future of Powys lies in tourism and hi-tech innovative industry, and a start has been made, which sums up the forward thinking of 'new' Powys. Renewable energy sources are at the forefront, as we can see at Llandinau with the largest electricity-generating wind-farm in Europe - its 103 turbines with a height of 150 feet have an uncanny affinity with Stonehenge.

The Centre for Alternative Technology was created on the site of Llwyngwern slate quarry, near Machynlleth, which closed in 1951; the site was allowed to return to nature. Gerard Morgan-Grenville, the co-founder, recalls: 'In those far off days the place was something of a jungle, scattered with ruinous buildings from which birch trees grew in profusion. The golden leaves were falling slowly in the still air and the sense of timelessness struck me forcibly. In such seclusion, so far from the pressures under which most people live, I had the feeling that something new, some fresh and saner way of living might be demonstrated. Indeed, my search for such a site

had brought me to this beautiful and private place.' CAT is an environmental charity aiming to 'inspire, inform and enable' people to live more sustainably. A solutions-driven organisation, offering practical solutions to environmental problems, its key areas are renewable energy, environmental building, energy efficiency, organic growing and alternative sewage systems.

Modern-day travellers into Powys pass over the centuries-old and much-worn earth-mound barrier known as Offa's Dyke, created in the 8th century by King Offa of Mercia to keep the Welsh in their place. Legend has it that it was once customary for the English to cut off the ears of every Welshman they found to the east of the dyke, and for the Welsh to hang every Englishman they found to the west. We cannot argue with such an endearing myth - but we may ponder perhaps on what happened to the ears. Powys today is a more welcoming place which embodies peace and tranquillity, but it now also offers a mix of entertainment and intellectual pursuits. Newtown has the Theatr Hafren and Builth Wells the Wyeside Arts Centre, while Machynlleth's Tabernacl Chapel has been converted into a thriving arts and performance venue – Y Tabernacl. All these and more attract local and international audiences for a variety of events, from Mozart to alternative comedy and from folk music to dance and drama.

The photographs in this book were all taken before 1974, so that they relate to Breconshire, Radnorshire and Montgomeryshire from south to north. As the three counties all have their individual characters, it seemed logical to divide the pictures in this way.

BRECKNOCKSHIRE (BRECONSHIRE)

'The county of Brecknock is 106 miles in circumference, contains about 620,000 acres, is divided into 6 hundreds, in which are 4 market towns, out of which only Brecknock, ye Shire Town is represented in Parliament. Has 61 parishes and about 5,034 houses. The air is good but sharp, and ye Soil for ye most part hilly, having some pleasant and fruitful Valleys. The county affords plenty of Corn and Grass in Ye Vales, and Ye Rivers abundance of Fish, especially ye Wye and ye Usk, which are full of salmon, trout &c.'

Emmanuel Bowen, *Britannia Depicta*, 1720.

ABERCRAF, *Dan-yr-Ogof Caves 1937* 88017

This picture is wonderfully typical of Brecon. It shows the River Llynfell emerging at the base of the cave. In 1912 Tommy and Jeff Morgan explored the caves by coracle and candlelight; they crossed not one underground lake but four, with huge chambers of stalagmites and stalactites. In all they found 10 miles of underground wonderland.

◄ YSTRADGYNLAIS
The Village 1938 88705

This picture, taken just where the A469 road to Bargoed turns to the left, shows what a diversity of shops and amenities existed in a town of barely 5,000 inhabitants. On the left is the RAOB meeting hall with a solitary figure on the pavement in the ubiquitous flat cap. On the right are Arnott's the chemist's in the foreground, with Watkins' Drapery, Pegler's, and Matthew's hardware store behind; then, where the road narrows, the cinema.

◀ **YSTRADGYNLAIS**
The Canal Bank,
Cwm Geidd c1955
Y40013

The canal age of the 1790s has long since passed now, so that the old Swansea canal we see here is a peaceful spot for a family outing. Note that dad is keeping a firm hand on the little girl for safety's sake. This photograph was taken at the point where an aqueduct carries the canal over the River Geidd, itself a tributary of the Towy.

▲ **YSTRADGYNLAIS,** *Commercial Street 1937* 87900

George Lowe's butcher's shop has pride of place here, next to the emporium of T L Jones. Further down on the left, and beyond the two cars, a grocer sells Lyon's tea and Wills Star cigarettes. The little Austin 7, or 'Ruby', in the right foreground predates the photo by some 10 years – it is a 1920s model. The buildings have little to commend them, and the picture has a drab feel - perhaps the lack of sunshine amplifies this.

◀ **YSTRADFELLTE**
Porth-Yr-Ogof Cave 1936
87804

Actually this picture was taken a mile south of the hamlet of Ystradfellte at the place where the River Mellte tumbles into the dark mouth of this cave, which in English means White Horse Cave. As this is a pure limestone area, similar to the Peak District and North Yorkshire, the whole length of the Mellte is a magnificent spectacle of caves and waterfalls. The three men just visible under the limestone arch give a Lilliputian perspective to the scene.

▶ **SENNYBRIDGE**
General View
c1955 S620001

Here we have a distant view of the village looking east toward the Brecon Beacons. Note that this is still limestone country, with a verdant mass of trees and hedgerows. This is not entirely a cosy hamlet, as the MOD has a vast army training ground here covering 27,000 acres. We can see the army quarters in the middle distance below the limestone escarpment on the extreme left.

◀ **BRECON**
The Bridge and the Beacons 1899 44707

We go north again to the centre of the National Park and the best-known town in Powys. The Frith photographer must have been impressed, as he took many views of the area. In the foreground is the multi-arched bridge across the River Honddu, which lends its name to Brecon's Welsh designation – Aberhonddu. Brecon stands at the confluence of the larger River Usk and this smaller tributary, the Honddu, and thus it has two rivers which become one.

▲ **BRECON,** *High Street 1899* 44714

This town can be confusing for the visitor, as not only has it two rivers, but also two High Streets. They have a charming differentiation – 'High Street Superior' and 'High Street Inferior' - but they are the same street, with the name change at the town centre crossroads. Here on a sunny morning the shop awnings are already out, and a shadow lies in front of W & A Gilbey's wine and spirit shop. Pride of place goes to the new-looking Victorian façade of Lloyd's Bank decorated with window boxes.

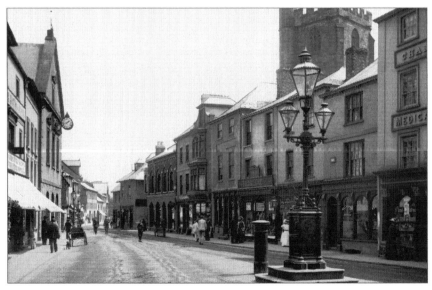

◄ **BRECON**
High Street 1910 62649

This is High Street Inferior, with the centrepiece of a fanciful wrought iron structure providing three gas lanterns as well as a drinking fountain. The Medical Hall (right) is a grandly named chemist's shop owned by one Mr Charles. Immediately next door is the building where the actress Sarah Siddons was born in 1755. Originally The Shoulder of Mutton, it later took her name, and has ever since been a variation on the Sarah Siddons Inn.

◄ **BRECON**
The Bridge and the Castle
1899 44717

Brecon Castle and town are Norman in origin, but the castle came first. It was the creation of Bernard de Neufmarche, one of many Norman conquerors, to keep the Welsh in their place. This site, on higher ground at the confluence of the Usk and the Honddu, was ideal. The castle saw plenty of military action in the ensuing centuries, but by 1800 it had fallen into ruin. The wealthy Morgan family of Tredegar Park came to its aid and rebuilt parts of the castle and the adjoining house in 1809. Its site, so useful as a castle, was equally good for a hotel - and the Castle Hotel it is to this day.

◄ **BRECON**
Newton Pool
1910 62663

Taken on a bright day, this shows Newton Pool pictured from across the water. We can see the boathouse clearly, and we have some activity in the pool. The pool is so calm that it reflects the oars, making a diamond-shaped mirror image.

▲ **BRECON,** *Christ College 1899* 44721

The history of Christ College falls into three unequal periods. For 300 years it was a Dominican friary; then in 1541 Henry VIII founded a school by Royal Charter. Finally in 1855 it became a public school by Act of Parliament. The chapel is a fine example of 13th-century work, though it was restored by Gilbert Scott in the 19th century. Of the cloister, chapter house and other monastic buildings nothing remains. Major new buildings were needed in the 20th century; all the features we see in the 1899 photograph were carefully duplicated, so that the modern architecture mirrors the original.

◄ **BRECON**
The Shire Hall 1899
44725

To give it its full name, the Brecknock Shire Hall is a very impressive classical-style building completed early in Queen Victoria's reign in 1842. The Assize Courts and Quarter Sessions were held here until 1971, and in 1974 it was converted into a museum and art gallery. The old courtroom fittings were preserved, and they can be seen with figures in period costumes when the museum is open.

▶ **BRECON**
*St Mary's Church
1899* 44729

St Mary's position in the centre of the town, and the dominating height of its splendid 16th-century tower at 90 feet, make it one of the most prominent buildings in Brecon. The Duke of Wellington stands high and mighty in the town's main square (centre), known as 'The Bulwark'. In keeping with the Duke is the imposing old coaching inn that bears his name, the Wellington Hotel (left).

◀**BRECON**
The Barracks 1910
62651

The military importance of Brecon continued into the 20th century and up to the present day. The barracks were built in 1805 as an armaments store, but many more buildings, including a hospital, were added in the 1800s. The 24th Regiment, based here, became heroes for their exploits at Rorke's Drift during the Boer wars in 1879: 140 Welsh soldiers held off an attack by 4,000 Zulu warriors.

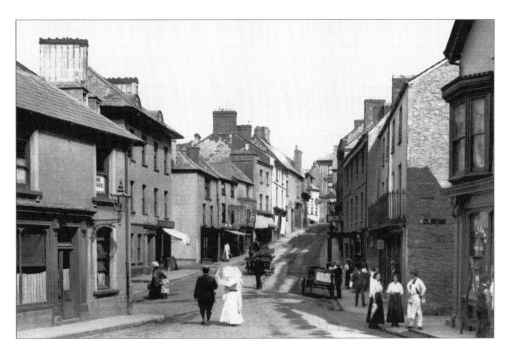

▲ **BRECON,** *Ship Street 1910* 62657

This street is a short one, running up into the town after crossing the Usk. The motor car is not yet a common sight, hence the horse-drawn carts going about their business. As was the fashion, everyone has a head covering with the exception of the youngsters outside the shop selling Allsopp's ale in the right foreground. If not a Sunday, the lady and gentleman nearest to us are surely in their Sunday best, he with his boater and plus-fours and she all in pure white with matching parasol.

◀ **BRECON**
Lower Ffrwdgrech
Waterfalls 1910 62668

As we have already seen, Breconshire is renowned for its many waterfalls and caves in the far south west. This is limestone country: the soft rock, assisted by the streams, forms magical shapes and contours as the water tumbles down. This view, taken on the private Ffrwdgrech estate, shows two parallel cascades plunging vertically into a secret pool. The two young girls sitting serenely atop the fall look almost posed, and indeed could well have been.

TALGARTH, *The Square and the Tower Shop 1938* 88475

Here we have a close view of Mr Evans' builder's and ironmonger's shop built on to the old tower, which was constructed in the 14th century. Next to the shop is a medieval-looking building, the home of the now defunct National Provincial Bank.

TALGARTH, *The Square 1937* 87702

We are looking up into the Square, with the National Provincial Bank, now in the shade, on the immediate right. Across the street are D L Edwards the grocer and the Ennis Hotel. Centrally placed, the town hall is bedecked with bunting and flags.

TALGARTH
High Street 1937
87701

The narrow High Street comes alive, not only with pedestrians and cyclists, but with the Union Jacks in abundance and in every shape and size. The photograph could have been taken around 12 May, the date of the coronation of George VI.

◄ THREE COCKS
The Hotel c1950
T343001

This amount of ivy is more than picturesque, it is also well trimmed. This cosy-looking AA hotel has two distinct types of window in addition to every conceivable style and size of chimney.

◀ **THREE COCKS**
*The Mill Stores
Café c1965*
T343029

Actually this fine
three-storied
establishment is a
three-in-one. The
filling station is to
the extreme left,
and then a café
and a bed-and-
breakfast complete
the facilities. The
age of the car has
now arrived, with
the front of a
Wolseley 4/44
peeping out
alongside a very
new Ford Anglia.

▲ **HAY-ON-WYE,** *The Crown Hotel c1955* H392078

Being so close to the English border, indeed partly on the border, this town was and is the
natural entry point into Wales for travellers and tourists. Hence, Hay has an assortment of
hotels; the brick-built Crown is of a high enough standard to warrant its RAC endorsement.

◀ **HAY-ON-WYE**
Broad Street c1955
H392056

Although one of the
busiest in Hay, this street
is also one of the
shortest. Here we have
the mock-Tudor Café
Royal, which was also a
baker, confectioner and
high-class grocer. We can
also see the signs of an
early traffic jam.

CRICKHOWELL
The Bridge 1893
32606

We are standing on the northern shore of the wide and shallow Usk, looking at the grand bridge. It is 17th-century in origin with 13 arches in total, but only 12 are visible from the west. To complicate matters further, only 6 are visible in this picture.

CRICKHOWELL, *The Castle 1893* 32609
Also known as Alisby's Castle, it occupied a high vantage point over the Usk. Originally built of timber, it was rebuilt in 1272. All that remains is a double tower; although still standing, it is now in danger of total collapse.

RADNORSHIRE

'The county of Radnor is 90 miles in Circumference, contains about 310,000 acres, divided into 6 Hundreds in which are 4 Market Towns & only one Radnor ye County Town privileged with sending 1 member to Parliament like ye rest of ye Welsh Boroughs, 52 Parishes & about 3158 Houses. The Air is sharp, the Soil barren & mountainous, abounding in Woods, Rivers & Moors, intermixed with some fruitful Valleys. Its chief Commodities are Cheese & Horses.' Emanuel Bowen, *Britannia Depicta*, 1720

CRICKHOWELL, *The Town Centre 1898* 41694

▼ **CROSSGATES,** *The Post Office c1965* C487008

A handsome brick building houses the post office and store in this tiny hamlet. Smokers had not become the social outcasts of today, as the Players sign affirms. BP petrol is also available, perhaps for the approaching Bedford Dormobile.

► **CROSSGATES**
The Llanbadarn Hotel c1965 C487005

This hotel looks so small that the description 'Bed & Breakfast' is more apt than 'Hotel'. The ivy growth and open windows indicate only one thing throughout Radnor, and indeed, Powys – and that is year-round moisture.

◀ **ELAN VALLEY**
Careg Ddu c1955
E185009

The four reservoirs of this valley were created between 1892 and 1903 from a 9-mile-long string of natural lakes to feed the demands of Birmingham. A viaduct carries the road across Careg Ddu and passes the grand water tower, whose purely functional purpose was for routine maintenance.

▶ **KNIGHTON**
The Knucklas Viaduct c1960
K61116

Ornamental towers at each end adorn the viaduct, which carries the railway over the River Teme into Wales. So close to the English border is Knighton that the railway station and hotel are actually on English soil.

► **KNIGHTON**
Broad Street c1955
K61043

Every conceivable example of architecture is visible here in the gently rising street, from The Norton Arms in the foreground to the clock tower in the distance.

◄ **BEULAH**
The Bridge c1935
B676003

Entering the hamlet, the main A483 crosses the River Camarch en route to Builth Wells. The waters were so shallow that a ford had sufficed for many years, and this bridge was quite new at the date of the photograph. The trees in the centre have been cut back for safety and to allow some light into the two houses.

▲ **BEULAH,** *Eglwys oen Duw c1935* B676002

The English translation is 'Church of the Lamb of God'; it was built in 1867. The exterior is in strictly Early English style, but the interior has a riot of coloured bands of brick and tiles on the floor. With a mosaic reredos and ironwork pulpit, it is a thoughtful and lavish Victorian interior.

◀**BUILTH WELLS**
*From Kington Road
c1950* B396029

Still travelling northward in 'the county of rivers', we see the River Wye lazily winding its way into the old spa town. Take care when looking for this place on a map: it is often marked by its Welsh name – 'Llanfair ym Mualt'.

► **BUILTH WELLS**
High Street c1955
B396061

After crossing the Wye Bridge, our man from Frith captured plenty of activity and detail in this photograph of the main street. The foreground has cars to the left and cycles to the right, the old facing the new as it were, whilst the trio of ladies yarning outside Davies Bros complete the picture.

◄ **BUILTH WELLS**
Park Wells c1950
B396034

This recreational area just outside the town would be newly laid out at this date. The shrubbery and flowerbeds look well cared for. A small detail in the left-hand building is the 'penny in the slot' weighing machine.

▲ **LLANDRINDOD WELLS,** *Station Crescent c1900* L145301

Victoriana and mock-Tudor set the scene around the unmade road of the Crescent. The large shop in the foreground specialises as a clothing and outfitting emporium. They would sell top quality textiles, as this was an opulent spa town at the turn of the century.

◄**LLANDRINDOD WELLS**
Middleton Street 1949
L145085

There is no such thing as an ordinary street in this town. True, the shops may have similar uses, but the Victorians made the most of the spa town by building wide, airy thoroughfares. The bounty of hotels and cafes, like the two shown here, contrasts sharply with the lack of pubs – pubs were considered too boorish for the town's image.

▼ **NEW RADNOR,** *The View from the Castle c1955* N169047

It was intended to link New Radnor with Old Radnor, two miles distant, to form a major city to be the capital of Radnorshire. The project faltered, confirming Welsh antipathy to large settlements.

► **RHAYADER**
The Claerwen Dam c1955 R348090

The mighty Claerwen Dam is pictured from the downstream side. Three years old when this photograph was taken, it is one of four dams in the Elan Valley which supply water to Birmingham.

◄ **RHAYADER**
The River Wye
c1935 R348032

The Wye frames the town centre, running in a loop around the western and southern sides. This was the scene of the Rebecca Riots in the 19th century, when local farmers disguised themselves by dressing in women's clothing to tear down the tollgates considered too expensive for the local workers.

► **LLANSANTFFRAID**
The Bridge 1888 20736

It is needful to give the full name of this hamlet –'Llansanffraid Cwmdeuddwr' - to distinguish it from at least five others with the same first name scattered throughout Wales.

LLANSANTFFRAID
The Church c1955
L342004

The meaning of the place name is 'church of St Bridget', which is the church shown here. Constructed by local workers, the church does not conform to standard architectural styles; the Welsh refused to follow the fashions of the age.

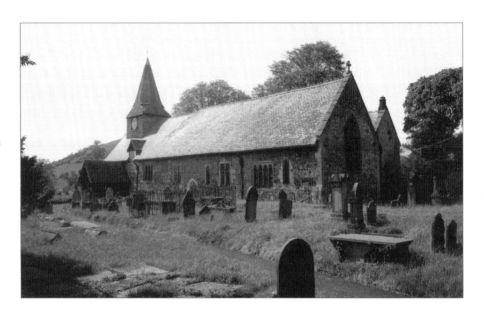

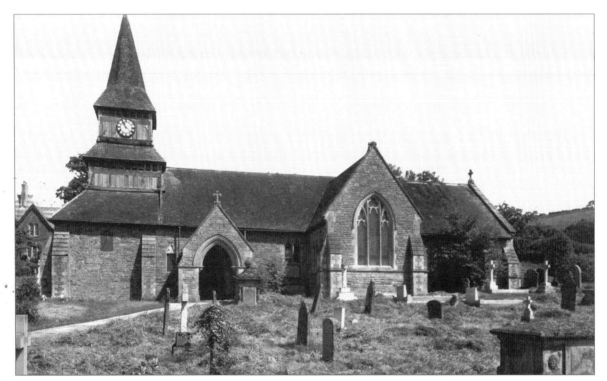

NORTON, *The Church c1955* N260001

The church is that of St Andrew, which lies on the western edge of a steep-sided valley, two miles north of Presteigne. There may have been a Norman church here, but most of its fittings were swept away in the restoration of 1868. A more apt description would be 'Victorian Gothic'.

MONTGOMERYSHIRE

'The County of Montgomery is 94 miles in Circumference, contains about 500,000 acres, is divided into 7 hundreds, in which are 6 Market Towns, and only Montgomery sends a Member to Parliament, which is the County Town, 47 Parishes and about 5660 Houses. The air is sharp and cold by reason of its high situation, the Valleys are very fertile, breeding very good Horses and plenty of Goats. The soil is stony, mountainous and rocky, intermixed with pleasant Bottoms. Its chief Commodities are Flesh, Fish, Fowl and all manner of Grain for the use of Man &c'   Emanuel Bowen, *Britannica Depicta*, 1720

LLANIDLOES *c1965* L403056

Llanidloes was famous for its wool and flannel industries from the 16th to the 19th century. In 1839, during a period of industrial depression and political unrest, it was the scene of a riot which lasted for five days until troops restored order. Over a hundred people were imprisoned or transported as a result. In the later 19th century the population of Llanidloes grew with the development of the lead smelting industry, which processed ore from the local Van and Bryn lead mines.

▼ **LLANIDLOES,** *The Market Hall c1965* L403055

The half-timbered Old Market Hall was constructed in the early 1600s, and is unique in that it is the only such hall in Wales still standing on its original position.

► **LLANIDLOES**
Long Bridge c1965
L403068

This bridge spans the River Severn, which rises in the nearby Hafren Forest from the slopes of Plynlimon (in Welsh Plumlumon or Pumlumon Fawr), the highest mountain in mid-Wales at 2468 feet. The bridge was built in 1826 by Thomas Penson, who also built Llanidloes' Short Bridge in 1850.

◄**NEWTOWN**
*From Bryn Bank
c1960* N171080

Despite its name, Newtown was founded in the 10th century. This vista from the heights of the Bryn looking over the town shows, in the far distant hills, that the fields were cultivated right up to the skyline.

► **NEWTOWN**
Long Bridge c1960
N171074

The River Severn is wide here on the approach to the town, so that a lengthy twin-arched bridge was needed to make the crossing. In typical Welsh tradition it was given a simple descriptive name.

► **NEWTOWN**
Market Day 1950
N171036

The market has not changed fundamentally over the years, except that today the emphasis is on clothes and general bric-a-brac, whereas the livestock sales that originated here are long gone. Overlooking the scene is the grand building and clock tower housing Barclays Bank.

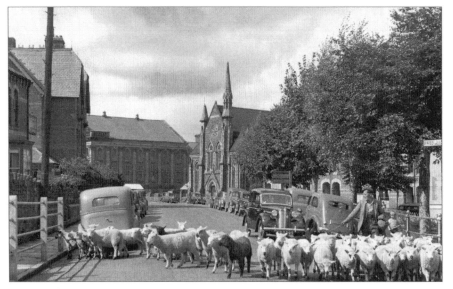

◄ **NEWTOWN**
New Road c1950
N171035

The old meets the new again in this picture. Horses have a statutory right of way over motor vehicles, but that is irrelevant to these sheep, who have made their own rules - the black car will have to be patient.

▲ **NEWTOWN,** *Broad Street c1950* N171016

Aptly named, this wide street wends its way down to the river. In the foreground stands the Bear Hotel, formerly The Bear's Head, built around 1868, with its mock-Tudor façade. In bygone times the hotel had a back yard in which strolling minstrels and poets would entertain.

◀ **KERRY**
High Street c1960
K144007

Brick buildings started to appear in the 17th century, when brick replaced stone and timber. The Herbert Arms (left) was originally Pen-y-Bryn Hall, built for Sir Edward Herbert of Montgomery Castle. The Mini on the right is very new, as the Mini Minor and Austin 7 went into production in August 1959.

MONTGOMERY, *From the Castle Grounds c1940* M286004

There are cynics who say that the remains of the castle are not worth the effort of the steep climb. Perhaps the climb is worth it for another reason: the view over handsome Georgian streets and the vast green bowl of hills around the town.

LLANFAIR CAEREINION
The Railway c1960
L394066

The Welshpool and Llanfair Railway still chuffs its way along the 8-mile narrow gauge line between the two towns. It used to be a bona fide railway, but today it only runs in the summer season as an attraction for tourists.

LLANFAIR CAEREINION, *High Street c1960* L394053

The Goat Hotel on the immediate right is still in business and a useful base for ramblers, but it is a bit small with only 5 rooms. The AA two-star rating may reflect the excellent pub food. The motor coach parked by the telephone box, is further evidence of the latter-day growth of tourism.

▼ **LLYFNANT,** *Cwm Rhaidr Falls 1892* 30276

Twin cataracts cascade down the limestone outcrop before joining together to descend almost gracefully forward and onward to tumble into the river, a thousand feet below.

▶ **MACHYNLLETH**
Pen-y-Bont 1901 46961

This town, known to its inhabitants as 'Mach', is situated at the far north west corner of Powys, so far that it is also in the Snowdonia National Park and 10 miles from the sea. The photograph shows the crossing into 'Mach' over the River Dyfi, or in English 'Dovey'.

◀ **MACHYNLLETH**
Penrallt Street
1899 44548

This street, which leads north towards Doll Street, the station and the river, was broad and quiet at the time of the picture. A lone horse and cart trundles up the hill, but the then unsurfaced road is safe enough for children to play in.

▶ **MACHYNLLETH**
Pentrerhedyn Street
c1955 M3098

This picture has several features to date it at around 1955. Firstly, the black car near the café is a 1950s or 1960s model, and the petrol pumps on the right are of that era. But the real give-aways are the large TV aerials, doubtless struggling to get any reception – Machynlleth is surrounded by verdant hills.

► **MACHYNLLETH**
*Maengwyn Street
1899* 44547

It is hard to imagine a town with a population of 2,000 being short-listed for the Welsh capital when it consists essentially of two intersecting streets. And this one, the Heol Maengwyn, also carries the main A489 road from the east. The street came to life, and still does, on Wednesday market day.

◄ **MACHYNLLETH**
Green Street 1895 37331

The Lion Hotel (left) has the strongest claim to immortality in this picture, all because Beatrix Potter stayed here when she visited the town as a young girl in 1888. She had this to say: 'Machynlleth a wretched town, hardly a person could speak English. Wynnstay Arms to which we were directed closed these two years. Lion, only other, a singular place. Welsh seem a pleasant race but I think awkward to live with'. The imposing clock tower stands 78 feet high; its full title is 'the Castlereagh Memorial Clock'. The architect was Henry Kennedy of London, and the clock maker a local man, Mr Edward Edwards. The clock was erected in 1873 by the Marquis of Londonderry to celebrate his son's coming of age.

▲ **MACHYNLLETH,** *The Avenue 1895* 36468

The town's connection with Owain Glyndwr gives it a unique place in Welsh history, as he was the last Prince of Wales to be crowned with the title. This was in 1404 near Parliament House, which is one of three medieval houses in the town. These houses in The Avenue are genuine 15th-century dwellings, and not to be dismissed as mock Tudor. Owain Glyndwr held his parliament in the town, thus making Machynlleth the ancient Welsh capital.

◄**MACHYNLLETH**
*The Corris Railway
1899* 44555

The railway was a working narrow gauge route running passengers up to the Corris quarries and bringing slate back. In 1948 it closed after a bridge was washed away, but it has now been restored to its former glory.

◀ **TAL Y LLYN**
The Hotel c1965
T277112a

This view of the hotel was taken from the lakeside. Today the building has been extensively refurbished, but care has been taken to ensure that all the 15 rooms have a lakeside view.

◀ **TAL Y LLYN** *c1965*
T277087

This natural, glaciated lake of 222 acres, its secret beauty almost hidden, lies north of Machynlleth, sitting right on the Gwynedd border of Snowdonia proper. In 1844 the late Colonel Vaughan of Hengwrt, the owner of the lake, built a small hotel. This was the Tyn-y-Cornel Inn and Hotel, and the good Colonel provided boats for his guests. An angler named John Henry Cliffe wrote the following in 1860, and I do not think it can be improved upon: 'Nothing in landscape can exceed the soft beauty of the Tal y Llyn; under peculiar lights – especially after rain or in lowering weather – the exquisite sight of the mountains on either side is perfectly magical. The contrast from the sublime to the beautiful leave an impression upon you which time cannot erase.'

▲ **LLANWDDYN,** *The Lake and Vyrnwy Dam c1960* L406043

Constructed during the 1880s, Vyrnwy was the first of the massive reservoirs of Powys. The village of Llanwddyn was drowned, but it can still be seen in times of drought when the water level drops. The village was re-built at the eastern end of the reservoir; its people received just £5 compensation for the loss of their homes.

◀ **LAKE VRYNWY**
Sunset c1955 L387013

We can appreciate the full four-mile length of the reservoir in this photograph. The 100ft height of the water tower is miniaturised, and the scene is not only breathtakingly beautiful but awe-inspiring as well.

▼ **LAKE VRYNWY,** *Llanwddyn c1955* L387004

This huge 19th-century dam, a monument to the engineering brilliance of the Victorian age, combines its functional role as a water supply for Liverpool with a touch of architectural genius. We can see the new site of Llanwddyn in the foreground.

► **STAYLITTLE**
The Clywedog Reservoir c1960
S621015

This reservoir was newly built when the picture was taken. The nearby hamlet of Staylittle allegedly took its name from a village blacksmith who was so quick at shoeing horses that his smithy became known as Stay-a-Little.

◀ **STAYLITTLE**
The Clywedog
Reservoir c1960
S621009

The reservoir's
prime function may
have been to fill the
perpetual needs for
water in distant
Liverpool, but it also
became a haven,
not only for bird life
but also for the
recreational
pursuits of the local
boating fraternity.

▶ **BERRIEW**
The Village c1950
B67401

A narrow bridge
crosses the River
Rhiw and leads the
eye to a group of
genuine black and
white Tudor houses.

◄ WELSHPOOL
Broad Street c1955
W471008

Lying in the valley of the Severn, the town does not seem particularly Welsh. Its original name was 'Pool', with the 'Welsh' prefix added to distinguish it from Poole in Dorset. The Victorian town hall and its dominating clock tower overlook some fine Tudor and Jacobean town houses. Meanwhile the collection of cars, bikes, pedestrians and perambulators and even a traffic light bear witness to the changing times.

◀ **WELSHPOOL**
View showing Powis Castle Gardens c1960
W471092

Designed by the Welsh architect William Winde, the castle gardens are spectacular. They drop down from the castle in four huge stepped terraces, and there is an orangery and charmingly precise topiary. The latter looks as if it is shaved daily.

▲ **WELSHPOOL,** *Church Street c1955* W471006

Advertising has always existed, though today it is controlled by the local authority. The van on the left was ahead of its time by using the back door for the slogan: 'If it's tractors ask Reginald Tildesley'. In the background is the turreted tower of St Mary's parish church.

◀ **WELSHPOOL**
Church Street c1955
W471003

As we look down from the church we can see the premises known as Corfield's Garage on the right, but judging from the mass of bicycles outside perhaps his sideline (or main line) was in the repair of pushbikes.

◄ LLANYMYNECH
Main Street c1960 L407009

The parked lorry belongs to Jones & Co, Corn and Seed Merchant; perhaps it is more than mere coincidence that a transport café is just across the road. In the far distance are Llanymynech Rocks, a 740ft-high limestone crag, which is now a nature reserve. The English border runs directly through the village, so that Welsh Sabbath drinking laws meant that on Sunday half was 'dry' and all the boozing was done on the English side.

◄**WELSHPOOL**
*The View from
Red Bank c1955*
W471002

The symmetry and
lack of individuality
in the houses to the
right of the
photograph point to
this being a modern
20th-century
housing estate.

▲ **CWM LLINAU,** *The Old Mill and the River c1960* C558008

Only a short river, the Llinau rises about three miles upstream from the site shown here, before
meeting the Tyfi. Barely a rocky stream, it appears to have produced enough power for the mill.
A sharp eye can detect the remains of a water wheel against the building, which would have
driven the huge millstones.

◄**MEIFOD**
*The Lower Village
c1955* M285037

A lone walker makes his
way along this pleasant,
rustic street. The large
house on the left bears the
sign Morgan, but from this
angle has no other
indication that it is the
usual general store.

MEIFOD
The Village c1955
M285019

There is everything you could want in one terrace of highly disparate buildings here in the centre of the village, from the whitewashed Midland Bank at the far end to some 'Players Please' at Rowland's store. The convertible car is a pleasing design, but inappropriate for the wet climate.

MEIFOD, *The Village c1955* M285013

Meifod lies on the main A495 road, which eventually ends over the border in Oswestry. There was not much traffic when this picture was taken; perhaps it was a Sunday, as the two ladies find the premises of M Williams closed (left) and the other couple farthest away are not in working clothes.

INDEX

FRITH PRODUCTS & SERVICES

Francis Frith would doubtless be pleased to know that the pioneering publishing venture he started in 1860 still continues today. Over a hundred and forty years later, The Francis Frith Collection continues in the same innovative tradition and is now one of the foremost publishers of vintage photographs in the world. Some of the current activities include:

INTERIOR DECORATION

Today Frith's photographs can be seen framed and as giant wall murals in thousands of pubs, restaurants, hotels, banks, retail stores and other public buildings throughout the country. In every case they enhance the unique local atmosphere of the places they depict and provide reminders of gentler days in an increasingly busy and frenetic world.

PRODUCT PROMOTIONS

Frith products are used by many major companies to promote the sales of their own products or to reinforce their own history and heritage. Frith promotions have been used by Hovis bread, Courage beers, Scots Porage Oats, Colman's mustard, Cadbury's foods, Mellow Birds coffee, Dunhill pipe tobacco, Guinness, and Bulmer's Cider.

GENEALOGY AND FAMILY HISTORY

As the interest in family history and roots grows world-wide, more and more people are turning to Frith's photographs of Great Britain for images of the towns, villages and streets where their ancestors lived; and, of course, photographs of the churches and chapels where their ancestors were christened, married and buried are an essential part of every genealogy tree and family album.

FRITH PRODUCTS

All Frith photographs are available Framed or just as Mounted Prints and Posters (size 23 x 16 inches). These may be ordered from the address below. Other products available are- Address Books, Calendars, Jigsaws, Canvas Prints, Coasters, Notelets and local and prestige books.

THE INTERNET

Already ninety thousand Frith photographs can be viewed and purchased on the internet through the Frith websites and a myriad of partner sites.

For more detailed information on Frith companies and products, look at this site:
www.francisfrith.com

See the complete list of Frith Books at: www.francisfrith.com
This web site is regularly updated with the latest list of publications from The Francis Frith Collection. If you wish to buy books relating to another part of the country that your local bookshop does not stock, you may purchase on-line.

For further information, trade, or author enquiries please contact us at the address below:
The Francis Frith Collection, Frith's Barn, Teffont, Salisbury, Wiltshire, England SP3 5QP.
Tel: +44 (0)1722 716 376 Fax: +44 (0)1722 716 881 Email: sales@francisfrith.co.uk

---

See Frith products on the internet at www.francisfrith.com

FREE PRINT OF YOUR CHOICE

Mounted Print
Overall size 14 x 11 inches (355 x 280mm)

Choose any Frith photograph in this book.
Simply complete the Voucher opposite and return it with your remittance for £3.50 (to cover postage and handling) and we will print the photograph of your choice in SEPIA (size 11 x 8 inches) and supply it in a cream mount with a burgundy rule line (overall size 14 x 11 inches). **Please note: aerial photographs and photographs with a reference number starting with a "Z" are not Frith photographs and cannot be supplied under this offer.** Offer valid for delivery to one UK address only.

PLUS: Order additional Mounted Prints at HALF PRICE - £9.50 each (normally £19.00)
If you would like to order more Frith prints from this book, possibly as gifts for friends and family, you can buy them at half price (with no additional postage and handling costs).

PLUS: Have your Mounted Prints framed
For an extra £18.00 per print you can have your mounted print(s) framed in an elegant polished wood and gilt moulding, overall size 16 x 13 inches (no additional postage and handling required).

IMPORTANT!

These special prices are only available if you use this form to order. You must use the ORIGINAL VOUCHER on this page (no copies permitted). We can only despatch to one UK address. This offer cannot be combined with any other offer.

Send completed Voucher form to:
The Francis Frith Collection, Frith's Barn, Teffont, Salisbury, Wiltshire SP3 5QP

CHOOSE A PHOTOGRAPH FROM THIS BOOK

Voucher for **FREE** and Reduced Price Frith Prints

Please do not photocopy this voucher. Only the original is valid, so please fill it in, cut it out and return it to us with your order.

Picture ref no	Page no	Qty	Mounted @ £9.50	Framed + £18.00	Total Cost £
		1	Free of charge*	£	£
			£9.50	£	£
			£9.50	£	£
			£9.50	£	£
			£9.50	£	£
			£9.50	£	£

Please allow 28 days for delivery.
Offer available to one UK address only

* Post & handling	£3.50
Total Order Cost	£

Title of this book . . . .

I enclose a cheque/postal order for £ . . . .

made payable to 'The Francis Frith Collection'

OR please debit my Mastercard / Visa / Maestro card, details below

Card Number:

Issue No (Maestro only):   Valid from (Maestro):

Card Security Number: Expires:

Signature:

Name Mr/Mrs/Ms . . . .

Address . . . .

. . . .

. . . .

. . . . Postcode . . . .

Daytime Tel No . . . .

Email . . . .

Valid to 31/12/12

Free Print – see overleaf

Can you help us with information about any of the Frith photographs in this book?

We are gradually compiling an historical record for each of the photographs in the Frith archive. It is always fascinating to find out the names of the people shown in the pictures, as well as insights into the shops, buildings and other features depicted.

If you recognize anyone in the photographs in this book, or if you have information not already included in the author's caption, do let us know. We would love to hear from you, and will try to publish it in future books or articles.

An Invitation from The Francis Frith Collection to Share Your Memories

The 'Share Your Memories' feature of our website allows members of the public to add personal memories relating to the places featured in our photographs, or comment on others already added. Seeing a place from your past can rekindle forgotten or long held memories. Why not visit the website, find photographs of places you know well and add YOUR story for others to read and enjoy? We would love to hear from you!

www.francisfrith.com/memories

Our production team

Frith books are produced by a small dedicated team at offices in the converted Grade II listed 18th-century barn at Teffont near Salisbury, illustrated above. Most have worked with the Frith Collection for many years. All have in common one quality: they have a passion for the Frith Collection.

Frith Books and Gifts

We have a wide range of books and gifts available on our website utilising our photographic archive, many of which can be individually personalised.

www.francisfrith.com

FF002068